# APPLE WATCH

*101 Helpful Tips and Secret Tricks*

**Take Your Wearable Tech Game
to the Next Level**

# Table of Contents

# Introduction

Congratulations on purchasing *Apple Watch: 101 Helpful Tips and Secret Tricks* and thank you for doing so.

The following chapters will discuss all things Apple Watch Series 3. If you are a tech-head or just a dedicated fan of the Apple Watch, then you probably already know that the Apple Watch Series 3 is the sleeker, faster, and more feature-packed iteration in the Apple Watch series. But, are you maximizing your use of this innovative device?

The huge leap forward in the Apple Watch Series 3 is its cellular capabilities that finally un-tethered users from total reliance on its iPhone pairing. The cellular feature brings with it a list of pros and cons, from the decision to incorporate an additional data plan cost to keep you running without total dependence on your iPhone, to the fact that cellular capability allows for fluid updates and notifications that seamlessly tie your iLife together. Automatic updates with Series 3 and crossover gear (think: AirPods, anyone?) create a personal relationship with the Apple Watch that supports the philosophy of better living through technology. Apple has clearly shown their hand in making a smartwatch that wants to make sure every aspect of your life is improved, managed, and entertained by tech. Nothing wrong with that!

Previous generations of Apple smartwatch made flipping through apps at the speed of life almost impossible and left users feeling that it was less the future they were wearing on their wrist, but a soon-to-be relic. Fortunately, Apple Watch Series 3 increased their confidence that their smartwatch is heading in the right direction. "It's fast, it's really fast," says CNET Senior Editor of Wearable Tech Scott Stein. "It's basically at the point where I wanted it to be three years ago" (Stein, 2018).

Don't fall behind! Dive into these 101 Helpful Tips and Secret Tricks to enrich your Apple Watch expertise and learn a captivating list of features to show off at parties. Nothing is a better conversation starter than, "Did you know my watch can do this?"

There are plenty of books on this subject on the market, thanks again for choosing this one! Every effort was made to ensure it is full of as much useful information as possible, please enjoy!

# Chapter 1
# Getting to Know Your Apple Watch Series 3

One of the best feelings in modern life is unpacking a shiny, new Apple product. If one thing has been consistent since the first iPod of the new millennium is that every white, beveled edge Apple design delivers that thrill of the future. The Apple Watch Series 3 is no different. The best way to start to hack this mini wonder of wearable tech is to make sure you have a firm understanding of its foundational components. If you have yet to make your wearable tech purchase, then you are in for a treat. If you are currently wearing your "squircle" faced watch, then reminiscence on that wonderful moment when you first unpacked, charged, and strapped it on.

This first chapter covers the basic terminology for the Apple Watch components and functions. Along the way, an introduction to the core decisions of setting up your Apple Watch is provided.

You are most likely already hip to the basics: the *side button* for power. Press and hold this button to turn on, and if already on, pressing and holding it will present button options to either turn off or contact Emergency SOS.

## Tip & Trick #1*: Did you know that you can bypass the need to click "Emergency SOS" by holding down the side button for only 3 seconds?

A countdown will begin, and you will hear an alarm confirming the countdown and a slider will appear asking if you want to end the call or not. If you do not deny the call, then Apple Watch assumes that you are intending to automatically contact emergency services. While this makes it more likely for someone else's tight grip on your wrist (or your awkward napping position) to accidentally call 911, this intuitive feature makes a helpful SOS call in a worst-case-scenario during a crisis.

*\*For this feature to work, you must be within the range of your iPhone's Bluetooth connection, your wifi is connected, or your cellular is on and supported.*

## Tip & Trick #2: Well, wait. I don't want to accidentally call 911. How do I shut down the SOS feature?

There are pros and cons to having automatic 911 (or your country's emergency number) calling features. If your watch does happen to call 911 accidentally, do not panic. It is better to stay on the line and explain that there was a mistake then to hang up. Hang-ups on 911 have to be assumed by dispatchers as an emergency and police will show up to where the watch is located. This removes resources from real emergencies and probably adds an unexpected and unwanted element to your day.

To turn off this feature, you can go into your Watch app on your iPhone, select My Watch, and then choose General. Under this menu option, select Emergency SOS to turn the Hold to AutoCall slider off. If it is active, this slider is in green. You will still be able to hold down the side button for 3 seconds and have the option to call emergency services with a slider option, but this preferences setting will eliminate an accidental 3-second button push as an automatic conversation with 911 if not caught in time.

That little scroll wheel above the side button has an official name, and it's very regal. You ready? This click wheel is the *digital crown*. This king of the watch's mechanisms can be utilized in two ways: as a scroll wheel and as the *home button*. When pressing the digital crown at its center, you are accessing the home button or the equivalent of the central button on iPhones.

The Apple Watch *screen* is the digital display for all of the watches' communications. It likes to be off to help save your battery life. Your screen will be off when you are idle. To illuminate the screen, it's as simple as a flick of your wrist! Otherwise, you can tap the side button, home button, scroll the digital crown, or tap the screen itself.

Once awake, your Apple Watch is ready to go. To view all your apps, simply press the home button within the digital crown. A honeycomb-like colorful display of all your apps should appear. This arrangement of apps is called *Grid View*. If Grid View is your visual organizing system of choice, then all you need to do is touch and drag to navigate to the icon of your desired app. If you prefer a more traditional list, then please meet your next tip and trick:

## Tip & Trick #3: Force Touch to Change Views.

Force Touch is when you touch the screen with more force than usual (like clicking and holding a traditional scroll pad on a laptop to left or right click). When you Force Touch on the Grid View screen, you will be presented with two options: Grid View and List View. Voila! List View achieved.

Within the more linear List View, you will be able to see the icon for each of your apps as well as their name. You can navigate through these by either scrolling the digital crown or by scrolling by touching the screen.

Next, meet your new favorite friend: *Complications*. What an odd name for such a useful tool. Complications are stored favorite apps that allow you to reload them without waiting for the whole app to reinvent itself upon every load. Complications hang out on your screen as an ever-present icon in one of three configurations: Circular Small, Utilitarian Small, or Utilitarian Large (these are smallest, small and square, and a long rectangular space, respectively). Complications are the widgets of the future. They allow you to keep your popular apps at hand and to keep these apps active with real-time updates.

## Tip & Trick #4: Set up your Complications.

Do this easily by going into your Watch app on your iPhone. Select the My Watch tab at the bottom left-hand corner and select Complications. Here, you can add or remove the apps you would like featured as constant icons on your watch face. Once decided, you can customize which icon is shown for the Complication and also its placement. To do this, go to your watch face and tap to activate its editing mode. Tap on the visible Complications as this should highlight only one of the icons. You can now scroll using the Digital Crown to see what different icons can be displayed. Hold and drag the Complication to reposition its placement and therefore display according to its Circular Small, Utilitarian Small, or Utilitarian Large status. Each watch face will have a different division of real estate for where Complications can be held. This setup is worth playing around with for a while until you find what works for you. These buttons will be your most used apps and tools. A good question to ask while deciding Complications is, "What are my goals by using this smartwatch in my daily life?"

## Tip & Trick #5: Use Complications wisely.

Utilitarian Large formatting allows Complications to provide limited, in-app data. This is useful for apps where you would like to have updates for on a regular basis such as: what your step count is, what the weather is like, how much money you are making on the stock market that day. If you religiously use your Apple devices for music, consider putting Now Playing as your Utilitarian Large Complication of choice. With this Complication, you can simply tap the Utilitarian Large area, and it will take you to the app player where you can control your music in an instant.

*Dock.* You know how, even with the best of intentions, you will open up one million tabs inside Google Chrome and then forget how you started with a mission to research intermittent fasting but wound up in a blog about tree farming in South Africa? Yeah, that's what your Dock is here for. Your Dock is where all your open and active apps hang out until you are ready to use them again or to remind you that you started an activity you forgot about in the middle of your Netflix binge. Your Dock is your patient best friend who lets you go on and on about your recent breakup and doesn't even bug you to change the subject! Access Dock by tapping the side button. You should see a portion of the app in your Dock with its most recent application status (how much money you have left in your Starbucks account, for example). Scroll through these with either the crown or your finger.

## Tip & Trick #6: Customize your Dock for faster app load by using favorites.

Make sure you are staying focused or up-to-speed on which apps are important to you by customizing your Docks setting. Do this by going into your iPhone. Launch your Apple Watch App on your iPhone. Tap the My Watch tab in the lower left-hand corner. Select Dock from the main menu. You can either choose for your Dock to display Recent apps, or you can customize your Dock list. Add to your favorites list with abandon. Remember, those apps stored in your Dock will launch more quickly and be easier to find on the go (without sorting through your entire app list).

## Tip & Trick #7: Don't waste time going from Dock back to List View or Grid View.

There is a Show All Apps button at the end of your Dock list. Use this. If what you are looking for isn't in your Dock, don't lose time (on a watch, no less!) backing up.

## Tip & Trick #8: Make sure your screen looks like what you actually want it to.

There are two ways to do this, one is easy and one which requires a bit more patience. Let's go over the slower method first. Remember Force Touch? Go ahead and Force Touch once you are on the home screen. This should send the entire home screen into relief and signal that you can scroll through watch face options. You can either select a previous watch face design or add a New design. If you click New, you can scroll through preloaded designs provided by the Apple Gods. Click a new watch face and boom. Easy peasy. To customize the features of your watch face on your watch, Force Touch your desired watch face, and then scroll left and right to highlight the different elements of the design. You can then use the crown to scroll through all the permutations (colors, size, style). It takes time, but you can do it.

However, by changing your watch face on your Apple Watch, you will not get a preview of the new watch face with any established Complications. For this faster and more accessible method, head to your iPhone and open your Watch app. Select the Face Gallery tab at the bottom of the app screen. This is a nice View All spread of available faces (rather than one-by-one on the watch). Once here, you can then customize your watch face. You can change the color for some, and you can assign where your Complications will go. Once satisfied with your customizations, just click Add. Pretty nifty, huh?

## Tip & Trick #9: Get rid of all those extra customized watch faces queuing up in one swipe.

Making a decision is hard, and having different options for your watch face may appeal to some, but it drives me nuts. For any Disney-fied or Modular watch face you are tired of coming across, go ahead, and press and swipe that face upwards. Apple is kind and asks if you are sure you want to Remove Buzz Lightyear. Click the Remove button and Poof! It is now deleted. You can also do this on iPhone within the My Faces section of the Watch app by clicking Edit and hitting the red Do Not Enter buttons by the undesired watch faces.

If you want to get extra-extra-customized, stay tuned for later in this guide.

## Tip & Trick #10: Know your Control Center.

Just like your iPhone, your Apple Watch 3 has a Control Center. The functions here are the meat-and-potatoes of your smartwatch functions. Control how loud, connected, water resistant, and bothersome your device performs. Get to it by swiping up on your watch home screen. In here you can:

- Check your battery life
- Connect to Bluetooth devices

- Mute your watch

- Control Airplane mode

- Toggle WiFi and Cellular connections

- Water Lock

- Silence Watch

- Enter Do Not Disturb

- Theatre Mode

The remaining components of your Apple Watch Series 3 include the microphone and speakers located stealthy on the left side of the device (of a left-wrist wearing user). The band that comes with your Apple Watch is obviously the band you will begin to despise within six months, but that is just the human aspect of falling in love and then living with your cool new piece of tech. Tips on dealing with this let down will pop up in Chapter 5.

Congratulations! You now have a solid beginning to understanding your Apple Watch. Now, let's look at the tips and tricks that will make your wearable tech useful, convenient, fast, and more fun.

# Chapter 2
# Maximizing Apple Watch Performance

One of the few pitfalls of the Apple Watch is its short battery life. Now, this is all relative, as the Fitbit can go for almost a full work week and then some while the Apple Watch Series is begging for a recharge after a day. However, the Apple Watch is the only smartwatch doing everything at once: fitness tracking, endless app options, messaging, GPS, and now, cellular. It kind of feels wrong to demand a robust battery for the sake of all these conveniences.

Regardless, you can go for the holy grail of running your Apple Watch with enough power saving tactics to maybe, maybe, go for two days without a recharge. It all comes down to your temperament. If making a nightly ritual out of recharging your devices is not a burden, then you can forgo most of these tips as dogmatic must-dos. Otherwise, use the tips and tricks of this chapter to manage the panic-inducing moments when you realize your watch battery is at its demise and you are scrambling to keep it alive just long enough to survive the long bus ride home.

## Tip & Trick #11: Invest in the GPS + LTE Apple Watch Series 3, even if you won't end up using the cellular capabilities.

There is a good reason for this: storage. The Apple Watch Series 3 with cellular has a 16 GB capacity. This is *twice* the amount in the Apple Watch Series 3 without LTE. If you are on the fence about spending more money because you are uncertain if you like the idea of adding to your data plan, think about the leap as an investment in your performance. More memory means more apps, faster processing, and a lot more options to customize your Apple Watch experience. The cellular capability is a nice option to have, even if you do not see its use at the present.

## Tip & Trick #12: Wake Screen on your schedule.

Go to the General menu, which is nested under your Settings app. You can customize your Wake Screen settings to better suit your preferences or your battery. To conserve energy, deselect any auto-wakes upon wrist flipping and audio app startups. It is a small change and may train you to tap your watch rather than bask in the automatic glory of a wrist flip, but it will give you more portable hours without a recharge.

## Tip & Trick #13: Turn off your watch without waiting for the Wake Screen.

If you are impatient or paying extra attention to battery life, make it a habit to use your palm to press flatly against the screen. This is an extra quick way to make your device sleep.

## Tip & Trick #14: Turn off your built-in heart rate monitor to spare battery life.

Apple Watch Series comes with a built-in heart rate monitor, which is a handy tool to get the real story on your fitness efforts. However, it uses too much battery. Go ahead and turn this function off by going to your Settings app, selecting the General menu, and scrolling down to Heart Rate Monitor. While it's noble to keep a tab on your ticker, this function is best left for intentional use during intentional workouts (and maybe not so much your trip to the grocery store). Don't worry, I assure you. Your heart is still beating even if this function is off.

## Tip & Trick #15: Easy battery saver: Choose dark watch faces.

When selecting your watch face, consider that the more there is to the design, the more light and as well as power that design requires. Black and yellow colors will save the most battery life.

## Tip & Trick #16: Power reserve will save your battery.

Make a habit of going to the Control Center (swipe up on your home screen) and checking in with your battery percentage (by tapping the battery icon). When you know you won't be maxing out your apps or anything watch-worthy for a while, tap on the battery icon and select Power Reserve. This is like Low Power mode on your iPhone. It will turn your smartwatch into only a watch (for the time being).

## Tip & Trick #17: Save more power by changing preferences for Reduced Motion and Transparency.

Go to your iPhone Watch app, open the General menu, and select Accessibility. Turn off the Reduce Motion and Reduce Transparency. This may take a little zing off of the watch experience, but you will benefit from not having to recharge every night.

## Tip & Trick #18: Turn on Grayscale to save battery.

Under the iPhone Watch app, the General menu, and then Accessibility, turn on Grayscale to enable black and white shading on all Apple Watch features. Arguably, taking away the colors of Apple Watch destroys the sense of fun. However, this is a good survival tactic if you are not able to recharge your watch for the foreseeable future and are just trying to make it home.

## Tip & Trick #19: Save power on your connected devices.

While in the Control Center, you can also select any connected devices and check in on their battery life. If you have AirPods connected by Bluetooth, you can then select the percentage display that correlates to their power level.

You can now select Power Reserve for your device. Amazing!

## Tip & Trick #20: Live in Airplane mode.

That airplane icon isn't just for when you are on a flight. Tapping Airplane Mode in the Control Center will turn off all radio transmitters from your watch. Think of Airplane Mode as the peaceful mode. Any connected devices, notifications, texts, interruptions from the outside world will turn off. This simple fix also temporarily spares your battery from background activities. Tap Airplane mode whenever you want to put a Do Not Disturb sign between yourself and the world. This can be an extra comfort when wearing such a connected device on your person, within your periphery, at all times.

## Tip & Trick #21: Toggle from Cellular to Wireless or go off the grid.

In the Control Center, you will see two icons, one that looks like the traditional wifi icon and the other will look like a cellular tower icon (a pole that is radiating waves from a ball at its peak). *Be careful! The Cellular icon looks just like some traditional Airplane Modes on Apple Watch Series 3.*

When these are both on, your Apple Watch will seamlessly go back and forth between wireless and then switch into cellular when the wifi is lost in order to maintain an uninterrupted signal. Make sure your Apple Watch is using a connection that you approve of by setting your preference. Cellular or Wireless options are on when the button is highlighted. To turn off a connectivity option, simply press to remove the function.

## Tip & Trick #22: Connect all your devices, even if you have no plan for all their uses yet.

Here is the one and only ringing endorsement in this guidebook for AirPods if, somehow, you have not already thrown them into your Apple Watch purchase. AirPods give you the freedom to use your Apple Watch Series 3 in the way it was intended: on cellular. You can take calls, listen to your music, and listen to secret voice memos while on-the-go. Go to the Control Center and select the Connect An Audio Device option (the triangle that radiates radio waves towards the bottom). Click this to connect AirPods, Bluetooth speakers, or any other audio accessory.

## Tip & Trick #23: Write custom responses for messages.

When you receive a message notification, you are able to scroll down a list of pre-written responses. You can add to this list of options very easily for frequent responses you think you will need. Just go into your Watch app on the iPhone, go down to Messages, and then get into Default Replies. Scroll down to click Add Reply. This is where you insert your best, "I told you to never contact me again" or other inside jokes you need at the ready.

## Tip & Trick #24: Slim down your app storage.

Unlike friendships, Apple Watch memory storage is not forever. Go to your iPhone Watch app and go to General. Then, tap on Usage. This will give you a profile of how much storage each app is using on your Apple Watch. Delete as needed. Start with the bigger downloads first, and see if there are any that you can depart with without too many tears. This will help increase the speed and performance of your overall watch experience. Also, check in and see which apps may be overlapping in their functions. If you have both the Strava and Workout apps to help track your running, make the call if you can live without Strava and still meet your metric needs. Workout, as it is factory installed hardware, cannot be deleted.

## Tip & Trick #25: Check in with Siri about your battery life.

You do not even need to pull up Control Center to check in on your battery status. Just go, "Hey Siri, what percentage is my battery?" Or some variation, and you will get a response in percentage.

## Tip & Trick #26: Check in with Siri about the battery left on your iPhone.

As there is no way to access this information from Apple Watch via an app or Control Center, it is a pretty great thing to be able to ask Siri, "Hey Siri, how much battery is left on my iPhone?" And get a percentage response even if you are miles away from your phone.

# Chapter 3
# Navigation & Notifications

The tips and tricks presented in this chapter are imperative to your stress-free experience of controlling your Apple Watch. As usual with Apple products, there is always a clunky way to perform an action, and then the intuitive (although often secret) fluid way to perform a function. This chapter highlights these fast-as-you-can options.

An almost existential question is also how to manage your notifications. Your Apple Watch can be your home base for reviewing these, or you may choose to refer to your iPhone to deal with the onslaught of communication and reminders. The good news is that you can determine how much you want to be bothered (I'm sorry, reminded) and by what.

Take care to spend a lot of time with these tips to build a strong navigational foundation. It will save you scads of time down the road when you would have to unlearn a built-in habit to get to the simpler solution. It is recommended to read each tip and then physically perform the task to make sure your muscles build the memory.

## Tip & Trick #27: What is that red dot?

No, it's not a bindi. A red dot at the top of your watch face means that you have notifications. Feel popular and then see Tip #39 to learn how to delete them all at once. You can pull down from this red dot to view your line up.

## Tip & Trick #28: Silence incoming calls quickly.

When a call is coming into your smartwatch, you do not even have to aim to hit the call reject or accept buttons to take action. You can just place your palm, lightly but firmly, over the watch face. This will silence the call automatically. The call will still continue, and you can then choose to take action, but the ringtone will be muted.

## Tip & Trick #29: Flip your view between an open app and the most recently used app.

A handy trick is to double click the home button within the digital crown, and this will flip the view back to your most recent app. Double click again and you'll get back to your current app.

## Tip & Trick #30: Zoom when you need to.

Skip going to your iPhone to adjust text size and use the Zoom feature on a case-by-case basis. Get into your Settings, then under General, and then under Accessibility, you'll find the Zoom status. Click this to turn it on, and now you can activate Zoom by tapping two fingers at once on the screen. This will Zoom the image, and you can scroll around by touching two fingers and dragging the view.

## Tip & Trick #31: Force reset when Apple Watch freezes.

Just like us, smartwatches have bad days. If your Apple Watch is struggling and is timing out, go ahead and hold down the home button within the digital crown and the side button at the same time. This will force your Apple Watch to restart and force a hard reset.

## Tip & Trick #32: Adjust Haptic strength.

Make sure you are comfortable with the Haptic strength of your notifications. Haptics are the light taps or vibrations that alert you, instead of sound, to a notification. Go to Settings, then General menu, and then tap Sounds & Haptics. There will be a slider bar to adjust the strength under the Haptic field.

## Tip & Trick #33: Choose what watch face you return to.

By default, after your watch has been asleep, it will wake up to the home screen of the digital clock. You can change this by going into your iPhone app and selecting General settings. Here, scroll down and select "Activate on Wrist Raise" to change the default option from Show Watch Face to Show Previous Activity. This will keep your watch work more in flow with where you left off.

## Tip & Trick #34: Boost your Haptic strength.

If the above adjustment is not enough, you can go to your iPhone watch app and select Sounds and Haptics. Enable Prominent Haptic slider at the bottom of the menu. This will maximize your physical alerts.

## Tip & Trick #35: Force Close an app without a hard reset of the entire Apple Watch.

On the rare occasion an app times out or stalls, you can force-close the app without restarting the watch. Press and hold the side button until you see the power screen options pop up with two sliders: Power Off or Power Reserve. Do not choose either and just go ahead and hold down the side button again. This will force close the current app and take you back to either your List View or Grid View.

## Tip & Trick #36: Press and hold down the Digital Crown to get to your home screen.

Quick, easy, done.

## Tip & Trick #37: Get in touch with your notifications.

Spare yourself from rummaging around elsewhere and go to the home screen. Pull down from the top to see your notifications. You can scroll through this one-by-one.

## Tip & Trick #38: Delete notifications one by one.

While scrolling through your notifications, when you come across one that you'd like to either ignore or just not review again, swipe on the alert from right to left. A

"Close" option will pop up to confirm the delete and press the X button to say yes. It's just like Tinder: swipe left to forget about it.

## Tip & Trick #39: Clear all notifications at once.

Maybe you are blowing up one day and need a break, or maybe it is just the normal course of having too many WhatsApp, Messenger, Facebook, Twitter, Instagram, and Email alerts begging for your attention. Practice serenity now by closing all notifications at once. Do this by going to your notification screen by pulling down from above on your home screen. Then, Force Touch anywhere on the screen. A "Clear All" option will appear and press the X to confirm.

## Tip & Trick #40: Prevent notifications from popping up in the first place.

For this, just go into your iPhone Watch app and tap on Notifications in the main menu. Enable the Notification Privacy. This will prevent notifications from popping up on your smartwatch. This may be a good tactic to take overall since you'll be greeted with notifications once back on your phone. You can keep your Apple Watch as a special "me time" timepiece.

## Tip & Trick #41: Go nuclear.

Want to start your life over? Well, the life of your Apple Watch, that is. Turn back time by going to Settings, then select General menu, and then find that Reset button at the bottom. Warning: This will reset all, and I mean all, of your Apple Watch settings. But sometimes, a clean start is the best way to turn down the noise in your life.

## Tip & Trick #42: Decide how you want to be bothered.

Notifications. So easy to love, so easy to hate. Go to your Settings app and select Sounds & Haptics. Sounds are self-explanatory, but Haptics is a fun change of pace. They are physical alerts in place of sound notifications (a light tap on your wrist).

## Tip & Trick #43: Make friends with Siri and set her up.

To activate Siri, just tap the home button within the digital crown. Now say, "Hey Siri…" and this will wake her up. A useful Apple Watch Siri command is "Hey Siri, Launch Settings [or any other app name]…" Saves you time from scrolling and swiping through your grid view.

## Tip & Trick #44: Tell Siri to sleep if you accidentally wake her up.

If you "Hey Siri…" and either change your mind or have become self-conscious talking to your watch, just say "nevermind" to cancel your Siri command. She won't mind.

## Tip & Trick #45: Hand Off your watch app to your iPhone.

Work seamlessly by picking up where you left off on your watch. All you have to do is start your iPhone and notice the icon at the lower left-hand corner. This should be an icon of the active app on your watch. Pull this icon up to access your unlocked screen. Enter your code or touch ID, then voila! Your open watch app is now in its exact same place on your iPhone.

## Tip & Trick #46: Save steps by using Quick Lock to better navigate apps.

If you want to go out of an app and back to a centered Grid View, you can tap the home button out, then tap again and then once more to re-center. Or, you can plant your palm over the watch face to activate Quick Lock. This automatically closes the watch. Then, flip your wrist to wake Apple Watch back up. Now, tap the home button and poof, you are back to a centered Grid View.

## Tip & Trick #47: Send messages fluidly with auto send.

Once you establish your reply, either default or a voice memo, you can just tap anywhere on the screen to confirm a send. You do not have to aim your finger at the miniature "Send" hyperlink text.

## Tip & Trick #48: Know when people messaged you.

Within the Messages app, just hold and slide the screen to the left in order to see the timestamps of each message. This helps you determine if you should respond ASAP or send a friendly reminder that you asked your dad three days ago if he wanted to go for a hike.

## Tip & Trick #49: Mirror your Do Not Disturb settings with your iPhone.

The Do Not Disturb function is a relief for those who need a notification break on the daily. If you go to your iPhone Watch App and select Do Not Disturb, you will see an option to Mirror iPhone. Enable this slider so that whenever your iPhone is scheduled for Do Not Disturb mode, your Apple Watch will be too. This saves you from repeating your efforts within the Apple Watch Settings menu.

# Chapter 4
# Hack Your Life: How to Utilize Apple Watch Series 3 to Improve Time Management, Fitness, and Self-improvement

The long game Apple is running is a bid on your full attention regarding all self-help projects. It is reasonable to say they are succeeding. Technological advances mean nothing if they cannot connect with the human experience. On one hand, technology is at a saturation point where there is nothing vital needed. You can now talk to someone instantly, by voice, video, or text. You can map directions, leave reviews, book reservations, buy almost anything, make travel plans, watch a movie, and plot your creative goals *all on your watch*. Further advancements feel indulgent, almost like they are gilding the lily.

This is where the Apple ecosystem excels. The vital space still in need of innovation is the eternal quest for self-improvement. How can you utilize your wearable tech to help you enrich your life? How can you interface with Apple Watch to better structure your day? These are not just conveniences but realized self-determined goals. Think of your Apple Watch as the bridge between your goals and accountability. The quicker you can reframe your relationship to the smartwatch as one that is part personal coach, part therapist, part personal assistant, and part motivational speaker, the richer your rewards will be. Technology is just a tool, yes. But, in the hands of Apple, technology becomes a personal revolution capable of changing your life.

Think small (as small as an Apple Watch app!) and take each tip one step at a time. These small steps and attention to detail will add up to form the bigger and brighter picture of a transformed you.

## Tip & Trick #50: Be on time.

What is the real point of having a luxury watch if you are going to be late? Oh right, it is super cool. Well, let's start with one of the virtues: Being on time. For most of us, it is a struggle. Go to Settings (this will be in your selected app display in either Grid View or List View). Tap the Time option. Here, you can add 5, or 10, or 30 minutes in the classic attempt to beat the clock. Go ahead and do it. Your mileage (and time savings) may vary.

## Tip & Trick #51: Know the weather to better plan your day by setting the correct city.

You can change your location for the Weather app by going into the iPhone Watch app, hitting My Watch, selecting Weather, and defining your current location. Adjust this for the city you are traveling to so you can pack better.

## Tip & Trick #52: Use Siri to set a timer.

"Hey, Siri, set a time for 45 minutes." You would be surprised, but this is the #1 app that smartwatch clad users go to every week. Maybe it makes some sense to keep track of time on a watch, but the usefulness of having a countdown when it comes to cooking, napping, completing chores, setting a work goal, setting a shopping time limit, keeping track of your reading and studying, or just reminding you how much time you have to diffuse a bomb cannot be overstated. Life happens in real time so get hip to how to make the most of it by using this favorite Siri command.

## Tip & Trick #53: Maximize the Weather app to get all the information.

Once open, the Weather app will display the weather in icon format. Tap the watch face, and it will rotate through exact temperatures in Celsius and Fahrenheit, then again for a likelihood of rain. If you Force Touch, you can get a button view of these options.

## Tip & Trick #54: Find your f#!$%*g iPhone!

Go to the Control Center. See that phone icon that has waves radiating from it? That is your new best friend. Tap the icon because that is the Pinging iPhone button. Your iPhone, wherever she is, will then audibly ping. Hold down this icon to emit bright flashes of light from your iPhone to relocate it after you accidentally let it fall into a deep, dark crevasse.

## Tip & Trick #55: Get your Flashlight on.

Go to the Control Center and tap the Flashlight icon. The screen goes white but dim. Not too impressive, eh? Flip the watch away from you, Apple Watch knows, and the illumination will increase. A handy little tip for when you are heading to the bathroom at 3 AM and do not want to wake the house.

## Tip & Trick #56: Get a customized Flashlight on.

Wait, there's more? Of course. Swipe left or right once in Flashlight to start a strobe function, or even to get a red light (easier on the eyes in the dark). For those fighting crime, use the former to deter your enemies. For those solving mysteries, use the latter to keep your sleuthing low-key.

## Tip & Trick #57: Do Not Disturb.

Get rid of all notifications or anything else that may disrupt your 14-hour writing marathon (you are working on your novel, right?). Click the moon icon in Control Center. Do Not Disturb will be set for the schedule as it is determined in your iPhone app. If you want to change or set a usual standard of 12:00 AM to 8:00 AM, do this in your iPhone now. Do Not Disturb and therefore, chill.

## Tip & Trick #58: Forget the Apple Calculator App and go for something that makes sense.

Having a mathematician on your wrist will always be useful. Go ahead and do not waste your time with the awkward factory calculator app that comes with Apple Watch Series 3. DialCalc is an ingenious solution that works with the limitations of the smartwatch UX. The clever app makes both numbers and functions live on a dial that you can rotate through to set up your equations.

## Tip & Trick #59: Avoid disappointment from browsing the regular App Store.

Wearable technology is still new and somewhat of a programmer's nightmare in making long-standing apps responsive in its microform. Make sure to only go on the hunt for watch apps from the App Store link from within the Watch app on your iPhone. This specialized version of the App Store only displays apps that are compatible with the Apple Watch Series.

## Tip & Trick #60: Theatre Mode to be a good citizen.

When you go and watch a movie or your child's school play, be kind and select Theatre Mode in the Control Center. These are the drama mask icons. In this mode, Apple Watch will be on silent mode, and its screen will not wake up unless you tap or press a button.

## Tip & Trick #61: Swim like a pro.

Now, this is cool. If you are like many of us humans and get the most motivated to work out when you track your progress and workouts with precise metrics, then Apple Watch Series 3 will get you gunning to jump in the pool. Go to the Control Center and click that water drop icon. This is Water Lock. It will turn off any watch response to taps or accidental button hits while swimming. To turn off Water Lock, you will have to turn the Digital Crown. When you do this, it turns off Water Lock mode and *ejects any water that may have filled the speakers during your workout.*

As always, when you add water with technology, there are some inherent risks. Water resistance can and will deteriorate over time. Utilizing Water Lock will help mitigate this wear and tear. Apple Watch Series 3 (and Series 2) is water resistant (not waterproof) with a water-resistance rating of 50 meters under ISO standard. This means that you can take your Apple Watch Series 3 for a shallow swim, a splash in the pool, and casual water activities. Any serious scuba diving (or deeper than a top-surface butterfly or backstroke) should not be attempted. Also, if you wind up in a body of saltwater, extra care should take place afterward. Wipe your smartwatch with fresh water and use a linen cloth to dry.

## Tip & Trick #62: Water Lock like a pro.

Go ahead and repeat Water Lock mode even after getting out of the pool. Remember that ejecting water function from your speakers? Spare yourself extra dry time and repeat until you hear a free and clear airway after several expels.

## Tip & Trick #63: Hike and bike like a pro.

One of the really cool new features of the Apple Watch Series 3 is the Barometer. This measures changes in altitude. This will benefit bicyclists and hikers as they can now include metrics about their elevation gains and descends accurately from just wearing their watch. Just access your Workout app or head to the App store (remember: within your iPhone Watch app menu) to browse elevation tracking apps.

## Tip & Trick #64: Workout with precision.

Go to the General menu, under the Settings app, and get into the nitty-gritty of how your workout tools are performing. For the most part, Apple Watch Series 3 will default to auto-detect Bluetooth gym equipment and to precisely track your runs (or well-intentioned jogs!) by only tracking while you are actually moving. There are workarounds by deselecting these options and using your workout apps. If you are worried about saving battery life, then opt for turning off the heart rate monitoring that is a built-in feature of Apple Watch Series 3 and will start tracking whenever your watch detects not just running but walking. By turning off the heart-rate monitor, you bought yourself the luxury of leaving auto-walk and auto-run detect functions on.

## Tip & Trick #65: Workout App is your friend in fitness, and you can add activities.

This app comes standard with Apple Watch, and it is one not to be ignored. Once you launch Workout from your App view, you can select various cardio activities you are about to participate in, and the app will track your caloric burn, effort, and progress towards goals. If you have an activity that you do not see in the selection, such as weightlifting, do not fear. You can select Other and rename the activity. This will now be saved as an option in the future.

## Tip & Trick #66: Make sure to integrate the Activity App between your iPhone and Apple Watch.

Your fitness progress report is going to show up in your Activity App, which is readily available on your iPhone. But make sure, if you are keen on using Apple Watch to improve your health, to select the Activity App as one of your Complications. The little bullseye icon will keep your metrics fresh within the mind, and the 30-minute exercise goal limit (that cannot be changed) in the app makes sure you maintain a healthy and reasonable daily goal.

## Tip & Trick #67: Beware of the Stand ring in the Activity App.

The innermost circle in the Activity app is supposed to track your standing time during the day. Unfortunately, Apple Watch Series 3 is most likely to count your sit time as standing time. Why does this matter? It may not to you, but for those paying attention to their daily output, it can be a bit of a bummer to get credit for calories burned that did not in fact happen.

## Tip & Trick #68: Set up Wallet to utilize Apple Pay.

I know, I know. The world is ending, and the banks know everything about us. And yet, there is nothing more convenient than not having to remember or lug out your credit card every time you have to make a purchase. Setting up Apple Pay is easy to do. You just have to add an eligible credit, debit, or prepaid card to your Apple Watch. Open the Watch app on your iPhone. Go to the My Watch tab in the bottom left-hand corner. Select Wallet & Apple Pay and follow the instructions for entering your card information. Your bank will be asked to verify if the card is eligible for Apple Pay and may require further verification. Once all is on the up-and-up, you are ready to use your watch to purchase goods and services in stores, online, within messages, in apps, and on transit. The possibilities! Basically, anywhere you can see one of these symbols the Apple Pay symbol or Tap to Pay symbol.

## Tip & Trick #69: Get to your payment card quickly with Wallet.

Avoid going through the hassle of finding the Wallet app, especially after you just ordered your medium latte with almond milk and there is a line of tired, grouchy customers waiting behind you. Double click the side button (not the home button) and your default payment card should appear. Hold this near the contactless reader on the payment machine. Wait until you feel a gentle Haptic (tap) on your wrist confirming the payment went through. Presto!

Depending on the machine, it may ask you to select debit or credit for processing your smartwatch transaction. Go ahead and select credit. Debit transactions may require entering your PIN as you would with a normal payment method.

## Tip & Trick #70: Pay with a different card than your default selection.

Very easy: follow the instructions above. Double tap the side button and then swipe right or left to browse through the payment cards you have on file through your iPhone.

## Tip & Trick #71: Save yourself time with online purchases and checkouts.

Make sure your billing address details are stored in your iPhone Apple Pay information. This way, while checking out and buying that sweet summer hammock on your smartwatch, all you will have to do is click "Buy With Apple Pay" and avoid the slow work of confirming where your bills go to.

## Tip & Trick #72: Set up Calendar in a way that makes sense to your brain.

Some people are more visual learners, and some people need information in the most linear way possible. Open your Calendar App and click and hold on the screen to adjust to your needs. The options you have are List View, Day view, and Today. If you click Today at the top of the app, it will link you back to a monthly calendar view and allow you to tap into any day of the week, month, or year.

## Tip & Trick #73: Let friends and family know where you are by quickly sending location information.

Within Messages, while you are chatting away with a buddy, you can easily share your location status by Force Touching the watch face. This will bring up three options, one of which is "Location." Tap this, and Apple Watch will let your buddy know which Starbucks you are currently waiting for them and how it was not the one further down the street.

## Tip & Trick #74: Stay in your zone even while playing music.

When you are using the Music app to play tunes, anytime you awaken your watch, the watch face will automatically display your Now Playing screen. This may be your cup of tea, but if you regularly let a playlist go and get on with your life, you can go to Settings, General, and then Wake Screen to adjust this preference. Turn off the Auto-Launch Audio Apps option so that you can start the music and then continue on with normal app use with no interruptions.

# Chapter 5

# Customization: How to Make Apple Watch Reflect Your Style and Personality

It is just a fact that you will use your Apple Watch more if it fits your style and personality. The worst feeling is wearing the somewhat bulky technical marvel and not feeling like it is a part of your lifestyle. This chapter cracks open the hidden options for customizing your watch display and common pitfalls to avoid when purchasing.

It is also important to set your security preferences so your watch does not seem like a stranger to you. It's a humble user. You can utilize the intuitive security features of Apple Watch to make sure access is a breeze.

Are you a Lefty suffering in a Right Hander's world? Do not fret. Apple Watch also provides the option to reverse wrist-wearing orientation so you, the more creative of dominant hands, do not feel left out.

Best practices also recommend culling your app list on occasion to make sure they are serving both you and your storage needs. Read on to start making your Apple Watch feel like home.

## Tip & Trick #75: Customize your watch face with your own photos and downloads.

If you have watchOS 4 or iOS 11, you can utilize photos on your iPhone as watch face design options. Start on your iPhone and use the Share Sheet. Get to your desired image and press the Share button. Then, scroll through and choose the Create Watch Face button. You will have two options, either a screen-filling Photos Watch Face or Kaleidoscope Watch Face. You can then customize the watch face as you did in Chapter 1. Lucky you on making the upgrade! Apple rewards you with more ways to be your unique self (and punish those hanging out still in iOS 10).

You can also change the watch face to a personal photo from the watch itself. Go ahead and tap the watch face to get into the editor, scroll right until you see New, tap the Add button, and then keep scrolling until the Preset options are run through, and you will start to see the photos available on your iPhone (as long as you are within Bluetooth range of your phone). It is a beautiful thing when you can make your own face, the face of time.

## Tip & Trick #76: Third-party Complications.

While the starter set of Complications are fine and dandy, did you know that you can add in Complications from third-party apps? The key is to get into your iPhone Watch app. From here, click Complications at the top of the screen and a list of already downloaded apps that are available as Complications will be displayed. Choose wisely! There is only so much Complication real estate on your watch face.

## Tip & Trick #77: Change the orientation of your screen to match with which wrist you wear your Apple Watch on.

Go to the General menu. General is nested under Settings (which is one of your Apps). Under the menu, tap Orientation. You can flip the function of the Digital Crown here, too, to accommodate a wrist flip.

## Tip & Trick #78: Passcode perfection.

Go to the Settings app, get into the General menu, and select Passcode. You can then determine some pretty handy customizations. If you turn Wrist Detection on, this means your Apple Watch will notice when you are not wearing your device and automatically lock your watch. Unlock With iPhone is another handy setting to keep on. This setting means that anytime you unlock your iPhone, it will also unlock your Apple Watch. This will save you the trouble of entering your passcode upon every smartwatch access point.

## Tip & Trick #79: Text you can actually read.

Access your Watch app on iPhone and select Brightness & Text Size. This might take some trial and error between selecting a preference and then giving it a test run to see if you like its effects. Know that adjusting via iPhone is the only way to manipulate these core functions.

## Tip & Trick #80: Buy the other watch bands. Yeah, I said it.

This is more of a morale booster than secret, coveted tip. If you are debating whether it is worth over the sixty dollar splurge on a different band, or maybe the same band or just a different color, go for it. What you are actually investing in is the usefulness and convenience of a larger expense. The idea is to make sure this piece of technology improves your life. If you dare not wear your model because it does not look appropriate for an event, or does not match your outfit for the day, then why even has it in the first place? Of course, Amazon offers deep discounts on bands from overseas, but you can try to order these at your own risk.

## Tip & Trick #81: Do not purchase the Ceramic Back Apple Watch Series 3 and pair it with a Stainless Steel band.

One of the most heartbreaking moments in owning a new piece of tech is the first incidence of damage. Whether it's a ding, a scratch, or a crack, it's a feeling of loss that is hard to not blame yourself for. Be warned, though. The Ceramic Back Apple Watch Series 3, which is only available on the Series 3 without cellular capabilities, is prone to scratching from metallic surfaces. It would go to reason then that placing a stainless steel, svelte-looking band next to this porous surface will not end well.

## Tip & Trick #82: Arrange apps in the order you want.

Honestly, this technique is easier to edit while in your iPhone app, but you can do this in the watch. Just tap lightly (not a Force Touch) on your Grid View display.

You will then recognize the shaky, alive status of all the apps just waiting for your instructions. Drag and drop your apps to arrange in the pattern of your choosing. Go wild and organize by a color code scheme for a peaceful look.

## Tip & Trick #83: Delete apps you no longer want (from your Apple Watch only).

As always, you can only delete third-party applications and cannot delete the factory preset apps. Just tap lightly on your App view and activate the Shaky app-mode and you will see the small little Xs at their corners. Precisely tap these Xs to delete an app. The nice part is, this will only delete the app on your watch and not on your iPhone. You will receive a confirmation screen, so do not worry about the likely event that your normal-sized finger will accidentally hit the incorrect minute app.

## Tip & Trick #84: Line 'em up!

You can arrange your app icons in Grid View in a single file line. It may seem impossible, but a dedicated user can do it. Go into your iPhone Watch app, and get to the app Grid View settings menu. Go ahead and drag each icon, one by one, to latch onto the last outlier. It's soothing. It's like knitting, but for your eyes.

# Chapter 6
# Have More Fun: Personal Communication & Entertainment On-The-Go

It is a safe bet to make sure that you purchased your Apple Watch Series 3 not just to help streamline your life but to have a little fun. There are some smart preliminary steps you can take now to make sure that when you are ready to access your entertainment apps, they are ready to perform without a hitch. This includes making sure you have the right gear.

A necessary step to maximizing your Apple Watch Series 3 experience is to invest further into the Apple ecosystem with a pair of AirPods (image below). Now, yes, this is exactly what Apple wants you to do. And, yes, it feels criminal that Apple Watch will not un-tether itself from Apple gear. Just like an amusement park, once you are on Apple's premises, you are invested in the full experience and cannot compare prices with competitors or with their specs. The happy news is that AirPods are worth the $159 (£159) investment. These little guys will keep you seamlessly engaged with your Apple Watch and iPhone, let alone any other Bluetooth gear you would like to connect to your support grid.

One of the best features of the Apple Watch Series 3 is how it can keep you connected with its cellular capabilities even away from your iPhone. This chapter covers the best practices for communicating with your friends, making Messaging less of a headache, and unlocking the surprise features that make Apple Watch 3 the most playful iteration of its series.

## Tip & Trick #85: Field incoming calls with more options than just Accept and Reject.

An incoming phone call can induce panic in some and annoyance in others. If you are one of the few still partial to the lost art of phone conversation, then this is good for you. Otherwise, know that when an incoming call is being received, you can pull up from the bottom of the screen to display two additional options, Send a Message or Answer on iPhone.

## Tip & Trick #86: Group your friends together for faster group communication.

Spend some time and effort within the iPhone app under the Friends menu option. The order you place your frequent contacts and the blank spaces that appear under this option will be reflected visually within your watch app.

## Tip & Trick #87: Use Friends view to know which of your contacts also have Apple Watch.

Go to the Friends app and scroll through your dial of contacts. If you tap their profile picture, this will pull up options to message or call, but if there is a hand icon at the center bottom of the screen, this means your friend is also living the Apple Watch life.

## Tip & Trick #88: Watch face Easter Eggs.

An Easter Egg is a gaming term for a hidden event or fun surprise within a game. In here, if you double tap your watch faces, an animation will occur, specific to that design. Tap the world image watch face and get a tour of the solar system!

## Tip & Trick #89: Easter Egg Watch Faces.

Spend time with the Earth and Sun watch faces. If you zoom in or out on these watch faces, they seamlessly morph from the celestial body into the icon for your home screen app. Also, if you tap the Earth watch face into its Solar System layout, try double tapping the Solar System view to have the planets align with their names. It is a pretty cool feeling to have all nine planets (we'll still include Pluto, the dwarf planet) all lined up for you on your wrist.

## Tip & Trick #90: Start by playing your music from your watch by putting your music on your watch.

This time investment pays off three-fold in terms of convenience. Go ahead and open the Watch app on your iPhone, select Music, and then select which songs you would like to load on your watch. If you are mainly using your Apple Watch for music listening purposes, load everything. If you are only using your Apple Watch for workouts, then create some gym-engineered sweat song playlists to upload in order to save space. Select upload and wait for the magic to happen. Now, your songs will go with you wherever you go.

## Tip & Trick #91: Access more music controls.

Inside the Music app, Force Touch to view the controls for Shuffle, Repeat, Source, and Air Play. If connected to wireless or Bluetooth near your iPhone, you can change the speakers that are playing your music from your AirPods to your iPhone speakers. This is true for any additional Bluetooth speakers you may connect.

## Tip & Trick #92: Take pictures like a pro.

Your Apple Watch can assist you in using your iPhone camera better. Open the Apple Watch Camera app and you will initially get a view of whatever your iPhone camera is seeing. To view yourself through your Apple Watch, change to the front view camera on your iPhone and position the iPhone towards you. The handy detail is that the Apple Watch offers a timer so you can take arranged photos without needing to contact your iPhone. You can also just hit the snap circle on your Apple Watch and this will trigger the iPhone camera to take your best selfie. Use this function to take better fur baby photos as well! If you have a wriggly animal, you can pick them up and fool them into believing you are just hanging out for a snuggle fest, when in actuality you have propped your iPhone up and were only waiting for the best moment on Fluffy's face to snap a photo from your smartwatch.

## Tip & Trick #93: Skip using the in-app button to snap pictures.

That little button is small and cozy right next to the 3-second delay. Skip this exercise in precision and use the side button to snap a photo on your iPhone.

## Tip & Trick #94: Make Mickey or Minnie Mouse tell you the time.

Go to Settings and under the General menu, find Sounds & Haptics. Scroll down and make sure Tap to Speak Time is on. Now, when you tap your home screen digital clock, guess who tells you what time it is on the dot? Now, if they only do something freaky and get a Steve Jobs watch face going…

## Tip & Trick #95: Take screenshots!

Yes, so very simple and satisfying to do. First, make sure the function is enabled in your iPhone Watch app by going to the General under Settings and turning on the Enable Screenshots slider. Just press the digital crown and side button at the same time on your Apple Watch, and snap! The screenshot will be shared with your iPhone.

## Tip & Trick #96: Scroll through Messages quickly.

It can be a pain to use the digital crown to wind through a long conversation. Within the Messages app, instead of scrolling, tap the top of the app field where your conversation mate's name appears. This will automatically rewind back to the top of your conversation.

## Tip & Trick #97: Really tell Siri to go away.

If you are not in the mood, you can dismiss Siri with the voice commands, "Piss off!" or "Go away!" She'll buzz off accordingly.

## Tip & Trick #98: Customize the color of your Emoji responses.

In Messages, you can reply with Emojis as an option. Once this option is selected, you will see enlarged versions of common emojis you can swipe through. If you Force Touch on these large Emojis, it will change their color. Keep Force Touching until you land on the perfect shade of blue for your heart.

## Tip & Trick #99: Get to your Emoji history quickly.

If you are like most users, your Emoji palette has a favorite hit list. In Messages, reply to a chat with the Emoji option. Then, swipe left until you reach the far right screen. This will be a matrix of your most recent Emoji history to pull from. Quickfire those manicured nails and salsa dancing girl!

## Tip & Trick #100: Set your preference for audio responses within Messages to streamline your replies.

The dictation method of sending a response text can be a bit intimidating to the uninitiated, but the technology here is pretty outstanding. However, when using an audio response (vs. a default reply), Messages will ask you after your audio recording if you want to send a dictation of the transcript (text) or the voice memo. You can set your preferences within the iPhone Watch app so that Messages will always default to one method or the other. Just head to the Watch app, select Messages, and tap Audio Messages. There are three options in here. Select Always Audio for voice memos, Always Dictation for text, or Dictation or Audio, so that Messages always let's you choose.

## Tip & Trick #101: Use Scribble app to type out replies or anywhere you need notes.

Scribble is a fun app that lets you finger-draw a letter that it will then convert into a digital type. The extra hack here is to use the digital crown to scroll through possible word complete options after several letters. So, Scribble out b-o-o, and you might scroll to the get the correct auto-complete for the bookstore.

# Conclusion

Thank you for making it through to the end of *Apple Watch: 101 Helpful Tips and Secret Tricks*. Let's hope it was informative and able to provide you with all of the tools you need to achieve your goals whatever they may be.

The latest in smart wearable technology from Apple has put competitors on notice. FitBit, Huawei, and Samsung have been putting out smartwatches that rival, but do not yet exceed, the all-around capabilities and ease of what the titans of tech have thus far created. The Apple Watch Series 3 is jam-packed with features that finally run fast and, with the advent of Apple Watch's cellular capability, can follow your day without letting you miss a beat.

More than 35 million smartwatches are expected to be purchased by the end of 2018, finally signaling that the wearable device is here to stay as a main player in the tech market. Make sure you make the most out of your Apple Smart Watch by learning all the nooks and cranny features which separate the casual user from the informed citizen. By understanding the core relationship between Apple Watch 3 and its iPhone platform, you can circumvent delays and frustration by streamlining the functionality of your watch.

You can set up the preferences and connectivity to extend your battery life (one of the few setbacks of the Apple series). After getting a grip (and Force Touch) on how to navigate your wearable tech, you can unleash the little device's powerful secrets to improve your life. Hack your communication, your fitness, your time management, and most importantly, go have fun!

The 101 Helpful Tips and Secret Tips guidebook turns the stop-and-go smartwatch experience into the seamless, 360-degree iLife that Apple promised since 2015. The price of the Apple Watch is already an investment. Make sure you match that investment with the priceless understanding of knowing you are getting the most benefits out of your tech buck.

Finally, if you found this book useful in any way, a review on Amazon is always appreciated!